Abrams, New York

ABODE

SERENA MITNIK-MILLER
and MASON ST. PETER
with
MELISSA GOLDSTEIN

Photography by MARIKO REED

CONTENTS

INTRODUCTION

We'd recently moved in together when we secured the lease for General Store in December 2009. We fell in love with redoing the space. It was our first foray into making a space that we had complete control over: our first "ours." We came up with "General Store" because we wanted a succinct yet all-encompassing name that we could do anything with. We didn't even want a "the" in front of it—didn't seem necessary.

When we opened, we were very interested in supporting creativity in the community; we had all of these friends—really amazing makers and artisans and craftspeople and woodworkers—who made one-of-a-kind things for us to sell.

In the beginning, the more well-known designers we were into were not willing to offer us terms, and we were broke, so our inventory was what we had in our home that we could part with. We emptied out our kitchen, living room, and closets to add to a mix of ceramic planters, tea sets, a midcentury sofa refurbished by our friend Josh Duthie of Chairtastic, baby sweaters from France, and leather feather earrings made by a local artist. From the start, people reacted with interest and excitement. We were really surprised that we made enough in the first month to pay our rent and order more inventory.

Month by month, as we introduced more stuff to sell, we became more thoughtful about why we were choosing each thing. Looking back, it's clear that the success of the store had a lot to do with our being open to trying a variety of goods. We stocked the store the way we stocked our house: with new and vintage items and well-designed home goods. It emphasized a different way of living—with plain, simple, well-made, beautiful things but not just one specific style.

Often when people came to the shop we would hear them say, "I wish my home looked like this." And we realized that was a part of why they were interested—General Store spoke to a simplified and directed design aesthetic that they were striving toward, though they didn't know it yet. Back then, you could go to bookstores with galleries, sure, but there wasn't a store that we would go into and think: This is my vibe; this is it!

At that time, finding a unique handmade ceramic meant driving through the woods of New Hampshire or some such similar journey—it was pretty much unheard-of. Then there was a big resurgence in small-scale handmade everything—carefully curated craft fairs and new design magazines began to pop up. We went from ordering a box of things from Japan to sell, to driving up and down the coast, picking up ceramics, soap, candles, and custom small-scale furniture and design items directly from artists' studios—and stopping for honey in Jalama along the way.

Over the years we've become more educated (which is easy, considering we went into this retail business knowing nothing). The store has this wide perspective with a very thoughtful curation, and it attracts people because of how it's put together, with each piece given equal importance—a vintage ceramic and a new hand-built mug, an Edwardian-era dress and a fresh-out-of-the-box pair of clogs, just-released coffee-table books and timeless classics—all presented against natural wood with bright whitewashed walls.

When we finally got to the point of owning our first house—after renovating two locations of the store and living in several rented apartments together—we had years of pent-up desires for our living space, our longed-for abode. Of course, you can dream up endless scenarios, but you can't test them without something concrete: The process of rethinking our house, beginning by stripping it all the way back, crystallized our design beliefs and point of view. After sharing the renovation of our Topanga home on Instagram and seeing that people were interested in the details of what we were doing and why, we realized that vision was resonating.

At home and in the store, it has become about more than owning and appreciating one-of-a-kind hand-made goods; it's about figuring out how to consciously incorporate them into your daily surroundings. It can start with your favorite ceramic coffee cup and spill into the rest of your life too.

We don't pretend to have all of the answers. But we do think about it. A lot. This book represents the sum of all that thinking, whittled down to the doing. We hope it inspires you.

CHAPTER ONE

VISION

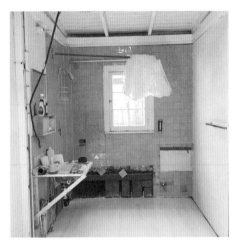

When we first stepped over the threshold of our Topanga home, it was so dark and masculine-feeling, it was like entering a cave—a cave with kelly-green laminate counters, ceiling joists painted cherry red, and a kitchen with two contrasting patterns of linoleum.

But so many other things called out to us: the exposed queen truss ceiling construction, the maple hardwood floors, the operable clerestory windows, the original doorknobs with a simple decorative pattern. Radiant light streamed into the enclosed sunporch in the back (inspiration to illuminate the rest of the house), and a giant century plant thrived outside—one of those agaves that only sends up a stalk every decade or so, toward the end of its life span. It was so real, this imperfect hundred-year-old, cabin-like house. And it had been largely untouched, waiting for us.

Honoring a structure's history and channeling its purest form lie at the heart of our design aesthetic. We knew just by looking at each other that we belonged here. We were in.

Over the years we've learned to seek out and value these marks of craftsmanship and originality, because we've had a lot of experience with stripping spaces back and building them up. When considered together, our tiny first apartment in San Francisco and our L.A. and S.F. stores checked every "must go" box: from dropped ceilings and nonsensical tiny rooms to moldy carpet and linoleum

Our Topanga house, from initial impression—note the unpainted fireplace, the linoleum floor, the red beams—to the early stages of being stripped back, when we first saw the open space and recognized its full potential

tiles adhered to black asbestos mastic. And then there are Mason's residential projects, spanning sensitive midcentury restorations to Craftsman bungalows and Tudor-style houses with modern additions.

These spaces are all inherently different, with singular purposes. But our approach has been roughly the same: Bring the site back to its essence, and incorporate only the things that are intrinsic to a successful space.

For us, the process usually starts with dreaming. We begin by brainstorming all the possibilities, and little by little we come back to reality, weighing what we can do logistically and what our budget will allow as we formulate a strategy. Learning to see potential is half of the challenge; making thoughtful choices after you've uncovered that potential is the other.

The open plan is an idea that we're always attracted to, but the degree to which open planning manifests is flexible. We understand that not everyone has the ability to knock down walls and move them around. People are limited by rental agreements, budgets, building codes, and circumstance.

That said, in this book we will encourage you to embrace the spirit of the open plan and promote flow as much as possible—whether it's taking out surplus doors, subtly dissolving thresholds between rooms, or just reorganizing furniture. We believe that living happily in a place depends on utilizing it to its fullest and eliminating anything that doesn't serve it from a practical point of view.

Mason's before plans (bottom) and sketches for our renovation (top) show our thought process for opening up the space, which included moving one part of the wall in the bedroom forward (and eliminating a door), expanding the bathroom by utilizing wasted square footage in the hall area, removing a door between the hallway and the main living area, and knocking down unnecessary walls in the main living area.

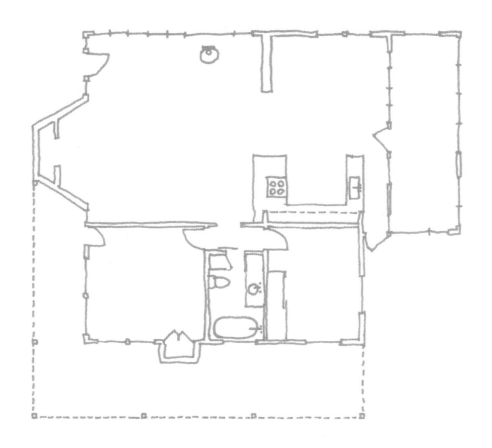

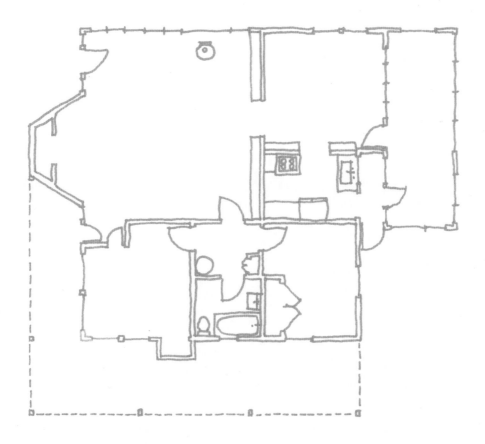

In these days of hyper-connectivity, there is a line of thinking that says that people crave their own distinct realms, where they can commune with their devices; houses with tiny, plentiful rooms are said to be in higher demand. We push against this notion. Ridding yourself of physical boundaries can be freeing; moving unimpeded allows for finding your own place and existing separately together; opening up sight lines promotes imagination, creating more moments for connection.

It's straightforward, really: You lose space if you have more walls. Take them out, and you gain.

Once we have maximized the opportunity for openness, we strategically tweak the environment. We bring in natural light (the ultimate mood lifter and design accomplice, making everything look effortlessly better); encourage indoor-outdoor living through extended decks or porches adjacent to common areas like kitchens or living rooms; and expose and introduce elemental materials, favoring wood, the most timeless material of all, stone, with its nuanced and hard-wearing beauty, and brass, a metal whose patina we are continually seduced by.

We peel back layers in pursuit of tactility and simplicity: removing carpet or paint from floors, trim or moldings from walls, tiles from ceilings. Where undesirable or disparate features cannot be cleared away, we apply a monochromatic finish—the great equalizer—unifying disjointed parts to become a whole.

Our Topanga house during its many phases of construction—from removing the tile in the bathroom, to ripping out the kitchen and living room walls, to painting everything white

Next, we introduce finishes that support functionality and keep the look as honest or neutral as possible. Even given these focused parameters, there are myriad options for any one material: We may treat natural wood with mineral oil; or apply a clear, water-based, low-VOC sealer; or bleach and whitewash; or simply leave it be, courting a natural patina. Often, we opt for a coat of white paint. Because we believe there is nothing quite like a coat of white paint, and choosing the precise shade is a master skill in its own right.

We also bring basic shapes into everything we do: Look closely at our work and you'll find circles, squares, and triangles—whether it's our store's logo, our skylights, custom shelving units, or drawer pulls. There is something about basic shapes' geometric balance and simplicity that we find incredibly compelling.

Finally, we add curating artwork and one-of-a-kind handcrafted objects with narrative from the local community—an approach we embrace in our stores and feel just as passionate about in our own home. We source furniture synonymous with quality: midcentury pieces in the tradition of Nanna Ditzel, Paul McCobb, Florence Knoll, Hans Wegner, Harry Bertoia, Ray and Charles Eames, Rudolph Schindler, and Richard Neutra; Shaker pieces conceived with utility and endurance in mind.

We like things. (We own two stores, stocked with pieces from many of our artist friends; of course we like things!) And yet, our aesthetic skews toward warm minimalism. It is a constant ebb and flow of editing and reediting and fitting together. We don't have it all figured out from the get-go. It is, and always has been, a process.

This book is our vision, distilled: the General Store way. And in the chapters that follow, we'll show you how to set it in motion.

The remodeled bathroom, featuring a bathtub gifted to us from friends across the street (complete with drawings by its original owner's kids), a salvaged marble slab for the countertop, a new cabinet by Mike Beavers, and hand-stamped Moroccan concrete tile

Our Topanga living room, where our dog, Macie, presides over everything.

CHAPTER TWO

DECONSTRUCTING

Every part of the process of making a space our own is our favorite. But this part, the part after the dreaming, and after the planning—the dawn of doing, of action—when you begin to dig in, get your hands dirty, strip away and rid yourself of unnecessary things to get closer to a simpler form: This part holds a very special, very therapeutic place in our hearts. Everything we do is in pursuit of the same goal: to bring out the essence of a space by balancing its elements in a visually harmonious way. Achieving this holistic result starts by being thoughtful about each part of the design.

With our first major project together, General Store's original San Francisco site, it was hard to know where to start. The space had been our neighborhood video store, which had gone the way of most video stores. Painted a minty seafoam green recycled paint shade you can get for free at the city of San Francisco's trash and recycling center, Recology, it had soggy, rotting carpet we suspected was once blue (but had grown so dirty it was now gray), linear fluorescent tube lighting installed in a low drywall ceiling, and a cramped floor plan in the back, divided into little rooms devoted to offices and X-rated rentals.

A look at how General Store's newest location on Irving Street in San Francisco came together:
from plastering the walls, to putting in the wood ceiling, to building out our circle shelf

HANDY STUFF

This is not a DIY book. This is a "how and why we do what we do" kind of book. But as you move through it, you'll find a few opportunities to get low-risk hands-on. In case you feel the urge, you should have a hammer, a Phillips-head screwdriver, a flathead screwdriver, pliers, a tape measure, a level, and a drill nearby.

It redefined the term "fixer-upper" and remains, to this day, one of the most revolting, cathartic, and satisfying experiences either of us has ever had.

In this chapter, we'll touch on the most fundamental structural changes you can make to your house to yield truly dramatic results: from taking down walls in order to improve flow and create an open plan, to stripping back floors, to opening up ceilings to expose your roof's framing.

Thanks to Mason's architectural background, we've felt emboldened to take on these tasks in a more cavalier fashion than others might—at times, to the peril of our sanity. That said, we always consult with a structural engineer before charging ahead, and we encourage you to do the same (full disclosure—we'll be reiterating the importance of this person throughout the chapter, so you may want to go ahead and just befriend one immediately).

We also recognize that these sorts of projects are not for everyone: For those of you who are renting, busting through the living room wall is not an option. Or perhaps your financial and logistical circumstances don't allow for disrupting your life in pursuit of a more authentic floor (we get it!). In these cases, we will outline less invasive courses of action for upgrading your space that will nonetheless have a big impact on your environment.

STRIPPING BACK WALLS AND FLOORS

If you're lucky, the path to renewed walls and floors is as straightforward as removing faux wood paneling and discovering flawless plaster, or pulling up carpet with a flathead screwdriver and pliers to find plain sawn, white oak flooring—our go-to—underneath. As with anything renovation-oriented, there are countless possible scenarios you may encounter once you start digging into the layers that comprise your space's history.

Keep a few things in mind before you embark on this journey. First, answer the question: Am I at liberty to make these changes? If you're renting, get the approval of your landlord before breaking through any surfaces (you may even find, as we have on occasion, that he or she will help you to execute your vision).

Second, consult with an expert, or two—a structural engineer and/or a design professional, depending on the task. If you do the initial investigating of the layers of your walls or floors on your own, choose an out-of-the-way area where you can do your detective work without creating an eyesore—a closet, a pantry, or, if you have access to it, a crawl space.

In our new San Francisco store, a stool by Ido Yoshimoto sits next to a door we hand-stripped using a heat gun. After scraping away the shiny brown paint that used to be there, we sanded the surface and left it alone: keeping the original door handle and functional locks.

A Word on Removing Walls

We've lost count of the number of times we've taken a sledgehammer to a wall and gone at it with all we've got. Understandably, you may feel the same desire—is there anything more thrilling?

But before you make any sudden moves, it's imperative to enlist the help of an expert to determine if the wall is load-bearing—a potential dealbreaker—and to help you to navigate around insulation, wiring, and plumbing. Once the wall is gone, you may need to take additional steps in order to unify your home's formerly separate spaces. A designer or contractor can help you to anticipate these, whether it's introducing a visual transition to bridge disparate design materials, or evening out incongruous floor heights.

Midway through every demolition project there is a moment when we almost want to leave the space as it is at that point—seeing the visual memory of things that have been removed, along with the building's inner structure, is always a thing of beauty.

"When I'm working with clients I tend to put on the lens of a preservationist—there's a budget, so I'm looking at the house and thinking: What's the least amount of work I can do to get the most effect? Removing a ceiling and exposing the inner structure of the roof is a great way to get more volume without adding square footage. You go from this contained space to this limitless-feeling space, because you've given yourself additional vertical height. Lighting will bounce around the interior in an entirely new way, and it will always feel brighter than it did." —MSP

EXPOSING CEILINGS

A vaulted ceiling with exposed beams, like the one we're lucky enough to have in our Topanga home, is elegance visualized. Old-growth lumber, put together with care by craftsmen—the design is pure, utilitarian beauty, with every beam playing a critical role (not to mention the bonus effect of the volume it adds to your space). Anyone who knows anything about ceilings will tell you it would be a crime to cover or paint it, because quite honestly, it's something that you can't really get anymore.

For us, that is as good as it gets. But prior to removing your drywall, ripping out nails, and submitting yourself to a possible torrent of granular roofing material, insulation, and debris that's accumulated over the years, you'll want to consult with a structural engineer to determine two crucial things. One: Will removing the ceiling compromise the structural integrity of your home? And two: Does your vision match the reality of your home's frame?

The structural supports we exposed inside the
original General Store are as much a part of
the space's personality as the things we sell.

A Quick Primer on Framing

The architecture of your ceiling is contingent on many things, including the year your house was built, the materials used, and the builder behind it. Still, there are some rules of thumb that cover popular scenarios:

If your house was built before 1950, there's a good chance it was constructed using the timber frame or post and beam style—both are simple, transparent approaches that differ only in the joints they utilize. They comprise vertical wood posts holding up wide horizontal beams (sometimes rough-hewn or hand-cut) that clearly delineate rooms. Over the years someone may have opted to add a dropped ceiling, covering the frame—in which case, when you remove it you will find something far better.

Our Topanga house is a perfect example of what seeing the structure and its supports looks like. The beams are a hundred years old, and the texture and the wobbly shapes inherent to the wood are all visible. Nothing is there for show, like drywall or trim, and the fundamental basics of the house are visible, rather than hidden away and made to conform to a square box.

We think it's beautiful for the same reason we think so many things are beautiful: because everything is working and nothing is "extra" or for show. And if it hadn't been painted red when we'd moved in we would have left it, because real wood (back when a two-by-four actually measured 2 inches by 4 inches, rather than today's nominal standard of 1½ inches by 3½ inches) is the ultimate desired probability. Its authenticity is rare and precious.

In contemporary roof construction the ceiling drywall is hiding manufactured joists—small, horizontal supports—and beams, which are basically a network of shorter, thinner pieces of wood around which the "guts" of the house—insulation, electrical wiring, and plumbing pipes—also live.

At General Store's San Francisco location, when we took away the dropped ceiling with drywall to expose the structure, we also exposed the unsightly electrical and plumbing (and lots of other unappealing stuff that had accumulated over the years, which we need not rehash here). The good news: The framing was beautiful old-growth lumber blocked in the X-brace style. So we redid the electrical to bring it up-to-date and painted the plumbing white to minimize it. The resulting industrial effect is a very specific "look," so you'll want to assess if it works in your space before committing to it.

Top: post and beam with simple truss. Bottom: conventional stud framing

SMALL CHANGES WITH LIFE-CHANGING RESULTS

Expose Windows

Dramatically scaling back window coverings—curtains, drapes, blinds, and valances—lets you use natural light to its full advantage, and, as we'll say over and over again: Bringing natural light into a space is the easiest, least expensive way to make it over. This not only creates a sense of spaciousness, but also flatters your interiors and alters your mood for the better.

For privacy, planting bushes and trees on the exterior of your home outside your window will also create a visual barrier, though it's important to be careful not to plant in ways that will block the path of natural light, thus defeating your efforts. If you don't want to pursue the bare-window route (due to privacy concerns or a need to protect artwork or other vulnerable items from the sun), there are other light-enhancing options.

In Wild's nursery, we reframed the windows (but kept the original glass) and opted to leave them bare to maximize light. Amazingly, he still sleeps until 7:00 a.m. The artwork is by our friends Thomas Campbell and Hillary Pecis.

"When we moved into our house, there were wooden blinds on every window. We took them off right away and left them bare: All of the spines of our books faded, but I prefer light with faded books more than dark with not–faded books. We also screen with plants: hanging succulents, ficus, and ferns in windows, and arranging them on benches under windows." —SMM

For smaller windows, we love a frosted film treatment on the window with a low-e coating that helps to deflect the potentially damaging effects of sunlight. A glass installation professional can brief you on the myriad options and install the film to avoid any rippling and ensure a smooth finish.

With medium-size and larger windows, we gravitate toward natural-fiber roller shades in canvas, cotton, linen, or bamboo, fitted to the opening—a simple look that adds warm texture. Serena has also sourced vintage linens from flea markets to fit over the windows, an approach we took in our son Wild's nursery.

And for floor-to-ceiling windows, we go for unbleached cotton drapes. A lot of times we end up using painters' drop cloths that we buy at the hardware store—if you run them through the wash a few times they change color a bit in a really beautiful way, and they sit and pool in the corner for a subtle, almost grand effect.

We screen our fireplace area with plants, both because it's a large, unfunctional space in need of green and because it conceals our cat's litter box.

"I like round incandescent lightbulbs—lightbulbs you can get at the hardware store. They usually come in two different sizes and two or three different levels of brightness. I will use the warmer LED bulbs if they are for a lamp where you don't see the bulb, but I have to be honest: I have not found many bulbs I like that are LED that I'm willing to look at." –SMM

Switch Out Light Fixtures

If we had a nickel for every fixture and bulb we've taken down (and stashed away in a box until moving day) in every rental we've ever lived in, we'd have enough money to buy a storage unit to house all of those unused light fixtures. We love to use frosted midcentury-style white globe glass pendant lights with lower-wattage bulbs—though feel free to experiment with shapes and transparencies—paired with low-profile porcelain or white powder-coated metal sockets: inexpensive fixtures you can get at the hardware store. You can, of course, easily change out a bulb yourself; if a fixture change is in order, consult an electrician on the specifics of your upgrade.

Open Up

A lot of homes have too many doors. The fact is, every little opening in your space does not require a closing—each room need not be physically sealed off from the others. When you remove an unnecessary door—say, one that separates your living room from your kitchen—it not only creates more space, but makes the space more functional.

REMOVE A DOOR

What You'll Need

Book/magazine/helper

Hammer

Flat-head screwdriver

What You'll Do

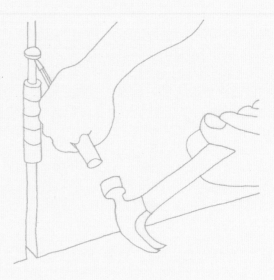

1 Wedge a book or magazine underneath the door to keep it from toppling over while you unpin it, or recruit a helper to hold it steady.

2 Force the pin up from the bottom door hinge. Taking a hammer and your screwdriver, gently ram the pin upward, using the flat end of the screwdriver against the pin and tapping the handle upward with the hammer until the pin lodges upward and you can remove it.

3 Repeat this step with the top hinge.

4 Remove the door. If you are renting, keep the door someplace safe until the time you are set to move out; if not, consider using it to make a spare work-table in your garage or elsewhere.

Simplify

We aren't big fans of overly fussy decorative trim and moldings, and we tend to remove them (see page 51) as a first order of business. That said, there are times when you remove a trim or molding and discover that the wall material doesn't quite reach all the way from the ceiling to the floor. In this case, we recommend installing a simple rectangular trim piece. Alternatively, if you don't want to remove the trim or molding, painting it the same color as your wall—as it is often painted an accent color—will help to lessen its impact.

In our newest General Store on Irving Street in San Francisco, we plastered the wall from ceiling to floor and chose not to add trim. Normally trim would cover the area toward the bottom of the wall where there are imperfections, but we'd prefer to see everything rather than mask it. The stool is by Josh Duthie, and the wall hanging is by Heather Levine.

REMOVING TRIM

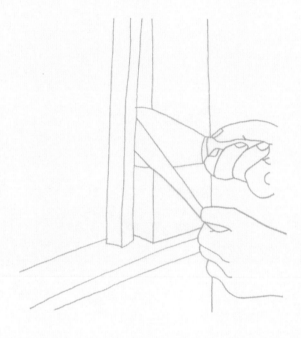

What You'll Need

Utility knife

Two 3-inch putty knives

Pry bar

Hammer

What You'll Do

1 To avoid unintentionally removing part of the wall with the trim, use a sharp utility knife to score the seam between the molding and the wall, cutting through the dried paint.

2 Slide a flexible 3-inch putty knife behind the trim and, keeping the knife there, wedge in a pry bar and pry the trim out a little bit. If you want to keep the trim intact and it seems like it may crack, insert a second putty knife between the pry bar and the trim. (If the trim won't budge, have a hammer handy to apply pressure by tapping end of putty knife lightly.)

3 Continue prying out the trim a little at a time down its length until the entire strip is free enough to pull off.

EDIT, EDIT, EDIT

Having begun this chapter with all things heavy lifting and made our way to less invasive projects, we leave you with the most accessible action of all: working with what you have.

Rearranging your furniture or rethinking the way it functions can be transformative. We recommend beginning with the living room—a space that often has the most flexibility and biggest impact when it comes to switching things up.

Start by sketching a basic floor plan, mapping out the existing furniture in your space in rough proportion to the size of the room. Looking at the layout from this perspective frees you to see all of the possibilities as far as where things can go.

If your current configuration follows the common layout of a couch facing a television (and watching television is not your priority for the space), consider a change. Our ideal orientation? Outside.

When a room doesn't have a view, then it becomes about creating a nice view inside: You can orient the room toward a beautiful piece of art or a bookshelf or the thing in the room that has the most character, like the fireplace. If it's a room where people are going to gather and talk to each other, you can facilitate this by orienting the room toward the center of itself.

Draw up new possibilities for the room, keeping in mind the goal to maximize flow of traffic throughout the space and ease of accessibility—you know a room has good flow when you enter it and know where to go and what to do. We place bulkier furniture

"I like to orient a room so that you're looking out a window toward a view or a garden, because it encourages people to engage with nature and with the outside. We positioned our sofa against the wall so that when you're sitting there you're looking out the windows opposite: You can see the trees, the mountains across the canyon, and the sky." —MSP

If you were sitting on our couch in the living room of our San Francisco apartment on the Great Highway, this is what you would see: an Eames chair, with the dunes just beyond.

close to and parallel with the walls, and keep sight lines undisturbed, reserving central positions for lower pieces. If you have a large open space, you can also use furniture in a way that divides the room and creates an intended path of travel.

This approach needn't be limited to the living room: One of the best things we've ever done in our own place was to rotate our fridge from south to east so that the door opens toward the wall as opposed to the middle of the room. As a result, the kitchen feels bigger and we don't have congested foot traffic problems. So. Much. Better.

Finally, if you really want a big change and you don't want to spend any money, get rid of things you don't love or use. It may sound obvious, but by taking a conscious look at your space with fresh eyes and being really honest with yourself, you'll gain not only in space but in quality of life.

This doesn't mean becoming a monk. But it does mean embracing change. You grow as a person when you put yourself through change that creates chaos and ultimately gets you back to a state of equilibrium. When we converted Serena's art studio in our San Francisco flat into a bedroom for Wild, we had to unpack all the stuff, go through it, and put it in a new room. That process forces you to weed out a lot of unnecessary things. The end result is that you have a new room, and you've seen everything that you have, edited it, and reimagined it. You don't have to move or spend any money to have a fresh perspective on how your space functions.

In Mason's residential project in Los Feliz, centering the dining room table (and the Park Studio light fixture that hangs above) helps to define the space, making for a natural progression from the kitchen without the need for a wall.

For Mason's Great Highway project clients, an open plan combines old, existing structural supports with new design, and a live-edge stair stringer adds a one-of-a-kind element.

CHAPTER THREE

ON THE SURFACE

You may have noticed that when it comes to design, we don't rely on color for impact. Serena's unofficial mantra is: The only option is white. That's not to say that we don't appreciate color— we have seen some amazing spaces that fully embrace all things bold and polychromatic—but it brings up an important point about our approach. For us, it's not about the wall, or the floors, or the counters or the cabinets. It's about everything together. We want to draw attention to the whole, not the part, and a cohesive neutral palette helps us achieve this.

It's something that's worth keeping top of mind at this phase of the process, when material layers come into play. Whether you're in a "now what?" situation, having excavated the strata of your existing floor and reached a dead end; or you're looking to harness the power of white walls; or you just want an easy upgrade for your lackluster countertops—it all comes back to the same idea: unifying your home and setting the scene for a tranquil, productive living space.

Our bedroom is essentially a white cloud of our own making, with linen sheets, a Victoria Morris bedside lamp, and a Noguchi pendant lamp.

BACK TO THE FLOOR

By now you've established the nature of the surface you're working with and are in a position of either refinishing your floor or remaking it. We'll deal with the former scenario first.

All wood fades over time. Sometimes it grays out, sometimes it can go very yellow, or, if your floor was the product of a remodel in the eighties or nineties, when it was popular to use a thick, shellacked finish, it may even have a glowing orange effect. Whatever the scenario, sanding your floor down and adding a clear coat is a great, easy step to dull the effects of all of the above. (FYI, while an engineered wood floor can only be sanded once or twice, a hardwood floor can be sanded multiple times—the exact number will depend on a few variables, including the thickness of the floorboards. Consult with an expert to find out the particularities of your floor.) There may still be remnants of the undesirable effect in question—but it will be significantly less obvious.

In our Topanga home we wanted a double-white effect. Our old maple floor had a mixed bag of ailments: Its finish was chipped, some boards were missing, several bits were raw, and other areas had been painted dark brown. After removing the damaged level through sanding, we bleached the wood (read: hired a professional to do it, as it is definitely labor-intensive). We let it dry for twelve

In the open space between our living room and dining area, a round skylight shines a spotlight on the labor of love that is our floor.

hours, then bleached it again, then let it dry for another twelve hours, and added a whitewash (a clear coat with white pigment in it).

This process is as light as you can go with your floors without just painting them white, which, of course, is also an option. If your wood floor is just too far gone and, even after sanding, still looks really patchy due to mismatched boards or the like (and you don't want to start over with a new floor), painting it white with floor paint is a great option.

Depending on your floor and how white and opaque or translucent you want to go, you can also do any combo of what we did with ours: whitewashing the floors and adding a clear coat, for a more translucent, subtler white; or bleaching the floors and adding a clear coat for something more saturated. The "after" will depend on your "before"—if, like us, you are starting with a dark floor, it will take more interventions to get it to a super-light place.

And if, unlike Serena, you don't care for white, you can add a gray wash, with or without bleach—or go dark, the total opposite direction. In that case, the beauty lies in contrast, so try an ebony stain, or paint your floors black.

A compare and contrast of wood and concrete floors, courtesy of our Topanga floor and the refinished concrete floor at our original store in San Francisco

A Word About White Floors (and Bad Raps)

White floors have a reputation for showing dirt. But in our experience, the lighter the floor, the easier it is to maintain. As far as dirt and animal hair go: You see it, so you clean it.

That said, white floors are admittedly trickier when it comes to liquids: A drop of coffee or even a water spill can become unsightly if not promptly removed.

Very dark floors tend to show everything, and are trickier to maintain. If your floor color decision is based purely on choosing a hue that hides the most, you are best off with gray.

Refinishing Concrete

If you have an existing concrete floor, either slab on grade (meaning the concrete has been poured directly onto the ground without a crawl space as a separator) or a topping slab, all you need to do to refresh it is to sand and polish the concrete and seal it.

You also have the option to add fades of color to the sealer to create a lighter or darker effect. If you unearthed the concrete beneath another material like tile, it may sometimes contain a "visual memory" or imprint: It's worth considering retaining this look and simply sealing the surface rather than sanding it.

If All Else Fails

Paint your floor white using floor paint, which is thicker and more durable, as it's intended for high-traffic areas. Got ugly-looking linoleum? Paint it white. Loud seventies-era tiles that mess with your scheme? Paint them white. You get the gist.

To reveal the concrete floor at General Store in Venice, which we polished and sealed with a clear coat, we first had to remove carpet and tiles glued down with tar.

NEW FLOORS

Here's a for-instance we get asked about a lot: You've ripped your floor apart and discovered that the buck stops with plywood. And you don't want plywood floors (not that there's anything wrong with plywood floors, for the record, which we'll address later on in the chapter).

It can be discouraging to go through the work of tearing apart your floor in search of a diamond in the rough, only to discover that there wasn't one to begin with—not to mention that the whole thing is going to cost you more money. The upside? This situation presents a certain freedom: the power to choose and invest in exactly what you want, rather than being forced to work with a choice someone else has selected for you.

It's also an opportunity to dissolve or establish new thresholds in your home—connecting rooms or blending indoors and outdoors by using a cohesive material and color; or introducing a threshold by virtue of a change of material (tile in the entryway, for example, where you ask guests to leave shoes or jackets).

Hardwood

With wood, the choices are abundant. Our favorite is hardwood white oak floor-ing, which is durable, long-lasting, and on the lighter end of the color spectrum. And though it's less expensive to work with thinner pieces, our size of choice is four-inch-wide continuous-length boards, because they are more consistent in appearance and less likely to look patchy.

The most common types of hardwood for floors are oak, maple, mahogany, and birch. Visually, there are subtle differences between the four: Mahogany is the darkest; oak, which also leans dark, shows more grain than its alternatives; maple is on the lighter, plainer, more uniform side; and birch is also light, with an inherent geometric pattern to it.

Keep in mind that wood looks dramatically different finished than it does un-finished, and time will alter its appearance. (This is an obvious advantage to using prefinished material, as you can see what it looks like before you install it. The downside is that prefinished wood tends to be engineered and, as a result, less sustainable and reusable.) People often stain wood, but just as we do when we refinish floors, we always prefer a clear coat or treatments that result in a lighter shade. Ask to see samples of aged wood from your carpenter or design professional so that you have a clear understanding of what it will actually look like over time.

When shopping for hardwood floors, it's a good idea to wet wood samples with water to see what they will look like when they are finished with a coating. Here, a few of our favorites: (A) mahogany, (B) oak, (C) ash, (D) beech, (E) poplar, (F) fir, (G) redwood, (H) birch, (I) cypress, (J) maple.

Concrete

Depending on how you do it, putting in new concrete floors can be prohibitively expensive. If your heart is set on this material, we advise a cost-saving approach that involves pouring a topping slab of concrete over the existing floor. This process offers the opportunity to add radiant heating by embedding tubing in the concrete—the most seductive, value-adding kind—an option well worth considering.

Tile

A versatile, water-resistant option for kitchens, bathrooms, entry spaces, and mudrooms, tile can add warmth and texture to a room. As a rule we shy away from bright, graphic tile in larger areas because it can overwhelm a space. Instead, we favor smaller tile, neutral concrete Moroccan tile, and matte white subway tile (an inexpensive, easy-to-install option).

Review your grout preferences with your installer ahead of time: Keep the lines as thin as possible, and match the color closely with the tile to create a seamless, flush appearance. (When you use a contrasting color for grout it emphasizes the grid over the material, which means you're looking at the grout and not the tile.)

Yes, white grout gets dirty. To fix this, you can use hard-core cleaning chemicals or scrub for days with all-natural hippie products (we use the all-natural hippie products). Another solution? Choose a colored tile with colored grout to match. Here, a few of our favorite tiles across the spectrum: (A) Heath Ceramics 4" x 4" Classic Field Tile, M18 Chalk White; (B) Heath Ceramics, M09 Chamois, Variation 3; (C) Heath Ceramics, M64 Steam, Variation 3; (D) Heath Ceramics, M01 Canvas, Variation 1; (E) Heath Ceramics Stan Bitters Tile, Recycled Clay Natural, Variation 5; (F) Heath Ceramics, M97 Alder, Variation 5; (G) Zia 4" x 4" Bishop Tile, Pink; (H) Heath Ceramics 3" x 3" Classic Field Tile, M18 Chalk White; (I) Merola Tile Boreal Quad, Matte White 2" x 2"; (J) Heath Ceramics, M46 Muslin, Variation 2; (K) Heath Ceramics, M61 Barley, Variation 3; (L) Heath Ceramics, M03 Parchment, Variation 5; (M) Badia Design 8" x 8" Hand Painted Moroccan Cement Tile; (N) American Olean 6" x 6" Starting Line Biscuit Gloss; (O) Heath Ceramics Stan Bitters Tile, XN Mixed Clay Natural, Variation 5; (P) Heath Ceramics, NW2 Natural White, Variation 2; (Q) Bliss Penny Round Matte White Tile

"I like wood to be unfinished, and I love the way that it looks over time when you touch it and it acquires a patina. To protect it, rub on a coating like tung oil that lets the wood breathe and live, as opposed to a coating that seals it." —MSP

Plywood

A very affordable option for flooring, plywood, if done well, can look very professional (and long-lasting too). Opt for clean-faced fir or maple plywood, which is sanded and finished with a clear coat of paint. You can buy a four-by-eight-foot sheet and have it cut into scalable, dimensional sizes to achieve a more conventional look if desired. Seal it with a low-VOC floor sealer like Bona ClassicSeal, to make sure it lasts.

Upstairs at General Store Venice, we covered the existing subfloor with clean-face Douglas-fir plywood and cut it into 1' x 8' strips to create a pattern.

COUNTERTOPS

How to solve the problem of counters that don't look the way you want them to? You can install new ones, of course. Our preferred materials are simple and authentic: marble, hardwood, or concrete. But if you don't want to go through the time and expense of starting over, you can employ a shortcut: Transform your counter by essentially covering it up. Buy the appropriate-size slabs of marble from a reuse or marble yard (which often has offcuts and remnant piles in standard countertop sizes), or milled wood (sanded and treated with mineral oil) from a lumberyard, cut to size so that it lies flush to your cabinets on top of your existing counters. The effect is akin to an oversize cutting board and can work wonders.

Rather than using a mitered edge on a client's marble countertop, which creates the illusion of a thicker material, Mason added a brass strip, filling the void between counter and cabinet and incorporating a unique transition between material changes.

Tile is among the least functional counter materials—it can't be used as a cutting surface and is hard to clean—so in our San Francisco apartment, we use an oversized cutting board to create a new surface. Opposite: For Mason's Noe Valley clients, marble countertops contrast cabinets with exposed-edge plywood framing and drawers made accessible by kerf-cut handles.

"Swiss Coffee by Behr is the color we have used in our home and in General Store Venice. It's a warmer white, which complements our scheme, from our eggshell-colored sheets to the light natural wood of our furniture. It's creamy and mellow on the eyes with slightly yellow-gray undertones, and pretty fail-safe." —SMM

"I use Benjamin Moore's Super White in my residential projects. We use a 1 base and tint with only titanium white—usually 4 ounces per gallon—which makes for the purest white without any color shift." —MSP

PAINTING YOUR WALLS, AND FINDING "THE ONE"

There are not as many shades of white as there are stars in the sky. But it can feel that way. If we were to pick a favorite, most versatile (and widely available) hue from the multitude, it would come down to two low-VOC shades: Swiss Coffee by Behr and Super White by Benjamin Moore. Be advised when choosing paint that different brands often have the same name for a color, but every brand has a different formula and so the actual hue will vary. Also, don't forget to add base. We recommend 4X base of titanium white to achieve the whitest white you can get.

A selection of Serena and Mason's favorite paints on the white spectrum, with input from our go-to painting expert, Stefan Simikich of Full Spectrum Painting: (A) Swiss Coffee by Behr (used in our Topanga house and General Store Venice), (B) White Dove by Benjamin Moore, (C) Swiss Coffee by Benjamin Moore (used in our Bay Abode rental property), (D) Cloud Cover by Benjamin Moore (used in General Store on Irving Street), (E) Ultra Pure White Gloss by Behr, (F) Chantilly Lace by Benjamin Moore, (G) Ultra Spec Pure 500, 3X Titanium by Benjamin Moore (favored by Mason for his architectural projects), (H) custom blend by Benjamin Moore (used in our Great Highway apartment)

4035

OPEN

COME IN

STORE HOURS
11-7 EVERYDAY

SHOP·GENERALSTORE.COM

4037

CASE FOR MAKING

WORK SHOP

11AM–6PM

CASEFORMAKING.COM

4037

Testing, Testing

When selecting your paint, keep in mind that the fluorescent lighting of the store will differ from your own environment. You won't truly know what a paint color will look like until it is on the surface in question, so it's prudent to test a color before committing. And, if you're going to go to the trouble of testing, it's best to select a good chunk of a wall—a patch that measures at least a couple of feet in each direction, so that you can really get a sense of it (forget the paint chips or swatches; they won't do the job). If you're deciding between colors, paint them right next to each other to see how they compare. In general, we use a flat finish on walls and a semigloss on doors, cabinets, trim, and anything that's not flat, to protect against dirt and fingerprints and scuffs.

As much as it might be tempting to make a decision in five minutes, give yourself time—at least a few days—to live with the color and witness the way it changes throughout the day so that you can make an informed decision.

And whatever shade you end up choosing, be loyal to it. Avoid the trap of using different shades of white to accent trim, or varying shades

We painted the rock wall surrounding the fireplace with Behr's Swiss Coffee, and the process was a true test of will. Because rocks are porous, and these rocks happened to be dusty and crumbly, we went through sponges, brushes, and all sorts of other tools before discovering what worked: a thick-bristle brush for dabbing, layering, and getting in the cracks.

of white from room to room. If you hire a painter, he or she may very well try to push you in this direction, but resist: It will compromise the potential benefits of monochromatic white—its calming, peaceful effect, and its ability to make less desirable elements fade into the background.

Make a plan for all architectural elements: If there is a support post in the middle of your space, painting it white is the best way to minimize it. The same applies to kitchen cabinets you're less than crazy about—choose a finish that will stand up to oil, grease, and all things culinary, like Insl-x Cabinet Coat. Another common element is a fireplace, which tends to be either nicely designed and worth preserving in its original state, or very much the opposite. In our house, for example, the fireplace was an afterthought, cobbled together with leftover B- and C-grade materials to form a crumbling rock wall. Painting it white helped to modernize it and make it less of an unsightly thing. If you are lucky enough to have a beautiful rock or brick wall that's really elegant and, say, crafted by a master mason, this is a different story. The decision to paint such a feature white is not easily reversible, so make sure you are 100 percent certain before proceeding.

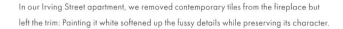

In our Irving Street apartment, we removed contemporary tiles from the fireplace but left the trim: Painting it white softened up the fussy details while preserving its character.

PAINT APPLICATION

Use new, clean instruments to apply your paint: a roller (a wide one for large spaces and a narrow one for smaller spaces) and brushes (for the details).

Ask to have your paint mixed and shaken at the store, and stir it gently yourself at home before starting.

Buy a separate material-specific primer to use for your base layer if you want your finished result to match the color in the can. (And, if you have a rough surface that needs evening out, hire a professional to apply a skim coat.)

Clean your brushes with hot water, and don't overload the brush so you can ensure an even application of paint.

Put down a drop cloth and tape the corners. Keep a wet rag or washcloth handy for wiping off drips, cleaning overloaded brushes, or saving any other surface you don't want paint on.

Finally, while we're big fans of improvisation as a rule, when it comes to painting it always pays to read the directions on the bucket. (There's plenty of time for artistic license down the road.)

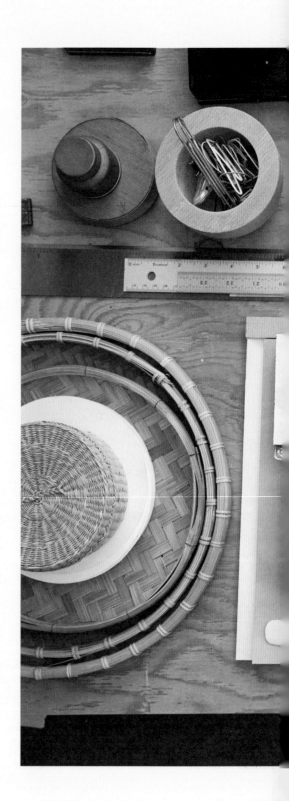

CHAPTER FOUR

REBUILDING

Everything in its right place; that's the dream.

When we begin to add to a space, we're constantly asking ourselves: How will this help functionally? How will it enhance beauty? How will we use it? The goal is to create an ecosystem that feels harmonious and effortless. But achieving that sense of "just being" can take a bit of doing.

In the weeks counting down to our son Wild's arrival, as we raced to finish the house, we left one of the biggest jobs for last: the kitchen. We lured our friend Ian Eichelberger, a master carpenter and general contractor, from his home in Hawaii to Topanga (sweetening the deal with the promise of a place to stay and daily Malibu surf sessions). He custom-built our plywood cabinets so that our appliances would be out of sight and we could maximize counter space, and helped us install floating shelves, made from beautiful planks of Monterey cypress that Serena sourced from Northern California wood broker Evan Shively of Arborica.

The result is one of the key focal points of our home, and no matter the chaos that envelops the rest of the place, it manages to stay relatively orderly: Our dishes and containers for coffee, tea, and dry goods line the bottom shelf. Our ceramics collection, including pieces by Rebekah Miles, Victoria Morris, Mt. Washington Pottery, and assorted vintage keepsakes, adorn the top one.

It's a great example of our philosophy in action, a twist on the tenets made famous by designers Dieter Rams and William Morris: Everything that's visible should be beautiful and useful; if it's just the latter, it should ideally be out of sight, rather than taking up premium real estate. Above all, any elements you introduce should support the above.

SHELVING

Our frequent ally in the quest to organize and display is the simple floating shelf, a storage scenario that allows for a visual connection to your belongings while keeping them out of the way. As with so many things, you have options:

1 A piece of wood with an L-shaped bracket—available off the shelf at most home improvement DIY stores.
Pros: The most basic, inexpensive, and easy-to-install choice, this is the ultimate do-it-yourself, instant-gratification scenario.
Cons: Because it's a mass-manufactured piece, it's not as special visually—you will see all of the hardware exposed in the finished results—and you're limited to the sizes and materials in the store. That's not to say this can't function and look great. It's all about where you put the shelf, the scale at which you are using it, and if you install it in a context that complements it—cleanly aligning the edges to an adjacent window, door, or nice piece of furniture, rather than just throwing it up onto an empty wall.

2 A vertical track that has an adjustable bracket and a wood shelf, also available at most DIY stores.
Pros: This affordable model can be transformed into something that looks like a floating shelf relatively easily, by gluing a piece of fascia board (ideally one that is the same species and the same length of wood as the shelf) to the front of it using a clamp, to hide the bracket holding the shelf.
Cons: Again, you're limited to what's available at the store in terms of lengths and types of wood. So if you want a ten-foot shelf and they only have an eight-foot in stock, you're getting an eight-foot shelf.

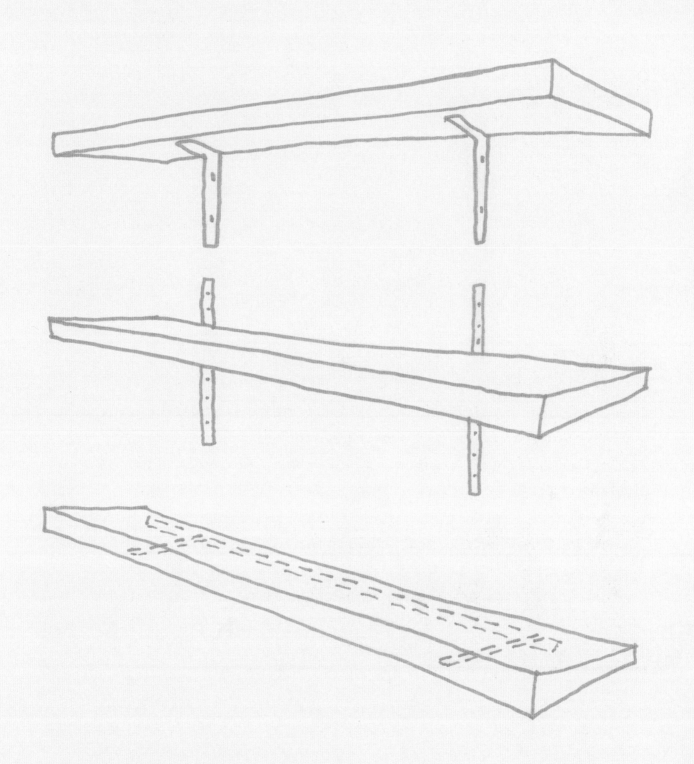

3   A metal bracket that you bolt onto the wall that is entirely hidden within the wooden structure of the shelf. This is slightly more of a specialty option, and something you're likely to find at a big-box design store.

Pros: This elegant approach won't require anything additional to hide its hardware, and is self-supporting after you install the brackets.

Cons: If the materials are not top-grade, the shelf can sag. (We've seen kits, for example, in which the shelf was made of particleboard and the welds on the steel bracket were weak, which means the shelf will wear out quickly if you put too much weight on it.) As such, it's worth consulting a woodworker and/or a metalworker to make sure you get the highest-quality pieces, but if you're going to the trouble to do that, it might make more sense to go with . . .

4   A custom wooden shelf that has routed-out spaces on the sides and the back, which you insert into a wood ledger installed onto the wall beforehand. (This is the option we used to make the shelves in our Topanga kitchen.)

Pros: You don't have to spend as much time and money on a metal frame, and your dimensions are limited only by the thickness of your wood—the thicker the material, the longer the shelf can be. That said, you should definitely have a professional do the construction of the piece and its installation, to make sure it is super solid and will last a long time.

Cons: You need to have supports on three sides in order for this model to work, and three sides aren't always available to support a shelf. (If you only have the wall behind the shelf and one to the side of it, it won't work.) Also, since we'd advise using only solid hardwood, this is likely the most expensive option.

If you'd prefer to forgo the above wall scenarios, there's always the free-standing shelf approach: attaching a custom bookshelf or existing furniture piece to your wall using a furniture anchor kit.

STORAGE

For us, storage is as much about creating an organized system for stashing things that are useful but not visually inspiring as it is about showcasing your favorite belongings so you can enjoy them on a daily basis, while keeping them out of the way.

Custom Built-Ins

There's a reason built-ins have long been beloved by architects of Craftsman and midcentury modern homes: They are ingenious ways to streamline design and provide much-needed storage. In our experience, this approach is best suited to a homeowner or a long-term renter, since it is site-specific.

We usually hire someone to create a custom, personalized storage solution using plywood: an easy-to-work-with, budget-friendly, and straight premanufactured material. (Despite our enduring love affair with hardwood, for this type of project it is not ideal, given the fact that the material is most widely available in rough-sawn quarter dimensions, is not always consistent with regard to its measurements, and can be prohibitively expensive.)

Mason's residential project in Los Feliz features custom Douglas-fir plywood built-ins. The seamless system conceals a fridge, laundry room, bathroom, and pantry.

Our custom self-supporting Monterey cypress bookshelf was designed by Serena and built by our friend Mike Beavers. We wanted something sturdy that would not only hold our books without flinching, but also divide the room and allow light to pass through.

Shortcut Solutions

Here is where we remind you to rethink the things you already have to suit your storage needs. Case in point: We had a square shelf unit that we were using vertically for books. We turned the unit horizontally, and it became an ideal spot to house our baby Wild's toys and double as a window seat.

And don't forget to look closely at your surroundings for site-specific opportunities: In our bathroom in San Francisco we set a reclaimed piece of wood on top of an already existing small tile ledge that spans the space between the shower and the sink. Adding the lumber has created a place on which to rest our shampoos and toothbrushes.

In Wild's room we turned a custom vertical bookshelf on its side to function as accessible toy storage. This photo was taken moments before Wild turned the peaceful organization back into a state of chaos.

In the bathroom of our Great Highway apartment, the existing tile
ledge was much too thin to hold anything useful, so we added a
piece of framing lumber to serve as a shelf and painted it white

Hooks and Pegs

When it comes to making jackets orderly or displaying your hat collection, you cannot beat a selection of hooks or pegs. They not only incorporate your things into your living space (rather than exiling them to a closet) but also create the appealing impression of organized chaos—an integral aspect of our design philosophy.

Our favorite hanging fixtures tend to be simple, hand-forged brass hooks or bent-wood and plywood versions (like the ones made by our friend the artist Josh Duthie) and Shaker-style knobs and pegs—so visually and tangibly satisfying in their solid simplicity.

If you are looking to create a design moment, installing a line or cluster of hooks will result in a composition with lovely visual rhythm. (Of course, one or two hooks are also ideal for suiting any storage needs in a small area—like equipping the back of your door to hold your towel.) When you put up hooks, you may be adding as many as twelve holes in the wall, so, as ever, it's best to be prepared: Map out the spots where you are installing ahead of time to avoid unnecessary marks. Hooks are also our go-to option for outdoor needs, since they are available in weather-resistant materials.

A Shaker-style peg rack, on the other hand, will only require two holes in the wall, but is more of a visual commitment, as you are essentially adding a hanging piece of furniture to your environment. You want to make sure that the aesthetic is compatible with your surroundings. We prefer the really long versions—six to eight feet—because if you are going to make this statement, it's best to really make it. The shorter versions don't tend to do the design justice, in which case, you're better off opting for hooks.

Because we have tiny closets, Serena relies on brass hooks in the bedroom for hanging hats, sweaters, and bags, among other things. If you decide to install hooks in your own home, be sure to check if your wall is drywall, in which case you need to find the studs before you start hammering.

A Building Block x Waka Waka peg (above) and wood hooks by Josh Duthie (opposite) keep things organized.

ADDING LIGHT

As we've mentioned earlier, there's no such thing as too much natural light. When adding to your environment, consider incorporating a mirror on a wall opposite your windows to further amplify available light. Also, if you do switch out your overhead and wall fixtures for frosted glass globe shades, as discussed on page 42, it has the bonus effect of distilling the light in a soft, ambient manner. Noguchi-style paper pendants will also do this for you. And if your walls aren't already a light color, painting them will make them appear larger and amplify the light within, as opposed to dark walls, which absorb light and tend to shrink the sense of volume.

But suppose you have done everything noninvasive that you can do to bring in natural light and yet still long for more? Installing a skylight or clerestory window will give you the most benefit for your buck.

"I'm drawn to the craftsmanship and the materials of Noguchi-style lamps because they are simple and delicate, and on the less-manufactured side. Even though we have a huge Noguchi Akari light sculpture in our living room, because of the material, and because it's a little bit translucent, it matches the nature of our environment and it's not overwhelming." —SMM

SKYLIGHTS

It's not the size of the aperture but its position that matters. Skylights come in operable, fixed, square, rectangular, round, and even triangular options—and, if designed well, they offer as much solar mileage from a two-by-two-foot design as a four-by-four-foot version.

Here, a checklist of things to keep in mind:

1 Be sure to get your skylight installed with a canted detail (which essentially means that it is angled rather than flat), as it will spread the light out over a larger area on your interior surface.

2 If you place a skylight on a roof toward the top of the ridge, as opposed to installing it at a lower angle, it will also spill more light throughout the space below.

3 If the skylight is facing in the direction of the greatest sun exposure (in the Northern Hemisphere that means southern or southwestern exposure), your light will be constant throughout the day.

4 A skylight's location with regard to your specific architecture is also critical to its success. A skilled professional can look for opportunities, such as putting a skylight up against a wall in your bathroom over your sink to wash the wall in light, bounce it into the sink and off the mirror, and diffuse it throughout the space as a whole.

A skylight over the entryway of Mason's Great Highway project floods the space with natural light.

Clerestory Windows

A row of windows set well above eye-level, clerestory windows add an ethereal warmth and glow to a space and rank among our preferred additions. What's more, they have a way of enhancing the perception of volume by creating a sense that the roof is floating. There are operable or fixed options, as well as clear and stained-glass iterations.

To determine if your space is a good candidate for these windows, first consult local code to make sure they are allowable, then hire a professional to investigate your home's perimeter and confirm if you have enough clearance at your roof level to bring in light. If your place, in true city-living style, abuts a neighbor's wall, you're unlikely to reap the benefits.

The handmade operable clerestory windows in our Topanga kitchen pack a double punch, providing both light and ventilation.

CHAPTER FIVE

OUTDOORS

THRESHOLDS

The choices are seemingly endless when it comes to selecting the perfect door for your project. These are a few of our preferred options:

1 A large-scale pivot door, which is designed with large-scale panels and hydraulic closing control, lending the most dramatic visual effect.

2 An accordion-style bifold door, enabling the entire wall to open while maintaining a more traditional, steel-door appearance than a sliding system.

3 A multiple hidden-pocket door, which opens an entire face of a building with external sliding doors that move into hidden pockets within external walls—or over the internal or external face of buildings to open a larger area. The sliding glass doors can be a single pane, multiple panels, or bi-parting, sliding into opposite pockets.

4 A split door, also known as a Dutch door, which you can open at the top while keeping the bottom closed.

5 A sliding barn door, which comprises one solid piece of wood that slides along the outside of the wall on an exposed track with visible hardware.

For as long as we can remember, we have both loved and longed for the outdoors. Serena grew up in Hawaii, spending most of her time outside and enchanted by the ocean—an ongoing muse in her artwork. Mason was raised in California, skateboarding, surfing, and hiking—the smell of the sagebrush in Topanga synonymous with freedom.

When we first opened General Store in San Francisco, we were thrilled to have a useable backyard. We wanted it to be a communal gathering space more than a place where we sold people things—somewhere to meet and just be.

We designed it together, and Mason built it out, with benches lining the perimeter and chunks of offcut wood offering places to perch. Serena picked out plants, befriending flea market vendors from whom she sourced vintage planters and succulents.

Our friend Jesse Schlesinger went to school at California College of the Arts and built a greenhouse with reclaimed materials for his thesis project. He'd had it in storage for a year, so on a whim we asked if he would like to put it in the backyard. He said yes, and we filled it with plants—more for the look of it than anything, but they sold quicker than we could keep them in stock.

It became what we hope for in any outdoor space: a picturesque place to be together, be comfortable, be inspired, and be closer to nature.

We made the conscious decision to keep the weathered siding on the back of the original General Store and leave it untreated. Mason built planter boxes along the wall, using reclaimed wood that continues the horizontal pattern.

Indoor Outdoor

Successful indoor/outdoor living often depends on dissolving the threshold that separates the two. The most high-impact way to do this is to engineer large openings by turning your wall into a door—which, if you are remodeling, can involve reengineering the structural support of the wall.

When considering the frame of your door, keep in mind that a steel or aluminum frame will be lower-profile, while a wood frame will likely have to be larger in order to support the span of a large opening.

Another approach to unifying the indoor/outdoor spaces is to keep the floor material cohesive and level on both sides. If your kitchen floor is covered in Moroccan tile, continue the scheme on your deck, creating the impression that you've doubled the size of the room.

And if none of the above is a possibility, focus on finding a way to enjoy the breeze, the light, and the sounds of outside while you're inside. The most obvious way to do this is to leave your doors and windows open during the day—which is our approach at home—and for us, this meant buying screen doors to keep out the bugs. We custom-ordered ours with simple wood frames and no cross supports (so that the view isn't interrupted) from our local hardware store.

Perhaps the most important aspect of extending the realm of the indoors is also the simplest: Create organic opportunities to gather, either by laying a rug and floor pillows down outside (the key is keeping these nearby so when the opportunity presents itself it's not a hassle), or by maintaining a supply of portable, weather-resistant furniture pieces that can be moved in or out with relative ease.

Mason's residential project in Los Feliz features an open sliding corner pocket door in the back, dissolving the threshold between indoor and outdoor. The back is an addition, while the front, pictured on the following page, is original. Painting everything white provides cohesion between the old and the new.

LANDSCAPING

California's natural landscape is a huge inspiration for us—we are always trying to bring together the Southern California desert with Northern California greenery. There are also several private spaces that have stayed with us: from the late great J. B. Blunk's hand-built house (which features a triangular-shaped back deck built into a hill) to Lotusland in Montecito, where the eccentric Madame Ganna Walska cultivated a wild aesthetic that brings every kind of plant together in one amazing place.

Noguchi's sculpture gardens are another reference point. His emphasis on the positioning of every piece in relation to the others, and the division of the space as a whole, is a reminder to cultivate smaller dialogues within a larger scheme, balancing angular planes, organic forms, and natural elements, and being mindful of the transitions between them all.

And we love to see the way people we know customize their spaces: Our friends and business partners Hannah Henderson and John Moore have mastered the art of maximizing a small space, filling their intimate yard with places for repose, including an outdoor couch mattress upholstered in weather-resistant material and perched on an oversize rock.

In the backyard of the original General Store, a custom redwood table by Luke Bartels is surrounded by seating in the form of chunks of eucalyptus and redwood. Weeds grow like crazy back there, so we laid landscaping cloth on the ground and covered it with rocks.

"My gardening style runs counter to my more minimalist interior instincts.
I'm inspired by variety, and I like a garden to be wild and disorganized—I
like my trees to be wispy and my hedges overgrown and trimmed askew. It's
about living out my design fantasies and letting myself go a bit." –SMM

In our own backyard, we've made a conscious effort to balance hardscaping (any nonliving elements, from rocks to built structures) with softscaping (plant life). It's nice to have smaller, more fluid elements to make up a transitional space that's not architectural (like a deck or patio). We favor drought-friendly wood chips and graduated rock on the ground rather than more common materials like grass, which requires abundant water and constant upkeep, or concrete, which has an industrial feel that can feel divorced from nature.

We began by placing a weed barrier on the ground—essentially a thick black cloth you can buy at any garden supply store to cover the dirt or sand and suppress weed growth. At our house we use wood chips because they match the rustic feel of our property, but we also love using rocks in graduated sizes. Regardless of your choice, be aware that everything will require some level of upkeep and replenishment.

Outside of Mason's Mar Vista project, olive and palo verde trees and bamboo are layered to screen the house.

GREENS

We are not experts in this department, but we are enthusiasts. We tend to favor succulents or any type of hardy, drought-tolerant ground cover, avoiding more finicky perennials, annuals, or anything that requires replanting.

In the temperate zone that we inhabit, certain plants fare better than others, so it's important to do some research about your own microclimate. Look around your neighborhood and talk to gardeners and people whose gardens you admire—like anyone with a passion, they will likely be eager to share their knowledge. There are usually small versions of every plant that you can experiment with—ask the people at the nursery what a plant requires to get a better idea ahead of time if it's a match.

Accept that there will be a bit of trial and error—we have straight-up killed many a plant that, on paper, should have thrived—but have faith also that plants are capable of comebacks: We once purchased an expensive string bean acacia tree from a plant shop in San Francisco and planted it in front of the store, where the wind from the ocean whips up and down the block. It almost gave up as a result, but once we moved it into the sheltered backyard it flourished.

OUTDOOR FURNITURE

In our yard, the furniture comprises a redwood deck with built-ins and chunks of offcut wood sourced from a wood broker and reimagined as outdoor stools and tables. Creating something similar is easier and less expensive than you may think.

Building a deck is a fairly straightforward endeavor for the DIY-inclined, boiling down to a process of measuring where you want supports to go, digging holes or placing foundation piers in the corners, and building a wooden frame—usually from redwood—with supports placed evenly below your decking material. Detailed how-tos on this subject are abundant, so if you're looking for a rabbit hole to go down, this could be the one.

As for the organic wood pieces, you can contact a wood broker or a miller, who tend to keep a pile of offcuts that they aren't doing anything with and will likely give you a good deal. If you're feeling more intrepid and budget-conscious, try contacting a tree-cutting company; some have great pieces left over from removal jobs.

Our custom stools in the backyard in Topanga are made by Ido Yoshimoto from eucalyptus offcuts.

Our preferred woods for this type of outdoor furniture include redwood, cedar, and eucalyptus, because they are well suited to the outdoor elements, durable, and age naturally without requiring finishing.

Our favorite designed outdoor furniture pieces include Donald Judd tables, benches, and seating (the market is also chock-full of pieces inspired by these originals), vintage wood deck chairs with a nice patina (not easy to find but possible to source at flea markets if you're persistent), handwoven cotton hammocks from Mexico, and outdoor mattresses—usually available for special order on their own, as opposed to part of a furniture set.

Also, rather than buying outdoor furniture, which is sometimes manufactured from cheap wood, you can tweak existing pieces to function outdoors: reupholstering a love seat or sofa in weather-resistant fabric (treated canvas is always a great option), or coating or waxing your own indoor tables or chairs with beeswax so that they resist water.

Indoor/outdoor space is essential to any successful contemporary living situation.
In the tradition of simplicity, this outdoor dining area functions both for gathering
and for creating a transition from deck to yard.

To complement a facade remodel for a project in Noe Valley, Mason designed a fence that functions as a permeable screen, allowing the clients to see out but also adding privacy.

ACCESSORY STRUCTURES

We believe that a house should fulfill your primary needs. But sometimes an accessory structure can resolve things your space cannot—be it storage, guest accommodations, or a place to work—and realize more whimsical ambitions while adding value to your property.

External add-ons are an integral part of our lives and practice: from Jesse Schlesinger's now-beloved greenhouse in the backyard of the San Francisco General Store to Mason's stilted office-cabin, built from reused wood.

The rules vary from city to city as far as the allowable dimensions of an accessory structure on your property, so before you start planning your office, potting shed, storage space, gym, art studio, or what have you, it's crucial that you consult the local municipality.

Your next consideration is to determine how best to orient the structure in order to achieve your maximum desired effect: whether it be taking advantage of views or exposure to light (in the Northern Hemisphere, a southern-facing position will maximize sunlight throughout the day) or ensuring a convenient connection to your house. The accessory structure should always be in dialogue with the main structure, so consider keeping the materials as similar as possible to ensure a cohesive look.

Mason's Topanga office cabin, a multi-use 10' x 12' reclaimed wood structure, is sited in a way that it turns its back on all other structures nearby, focusing its view on a creek and a hillside adjacent to it.

The now-legendary greenhouse in the backyard of the original General Store was designed
and built from reclaimed materials by our friend Jesse Schlesinger for his final project at CCA.

For his office, a large deck with a small structure on it, Mason sited the southern-facing structure in an oak grove with ample canopy cover and positioned it so that it turned its back on all the other man-made buildings nearby, focusing its view on a creek and adjacent hillside.

The interior is equipped with built-ins and lofted elements that help to make the most of the small space. This is perhaps the most important consideration if you're building a live/work structure, an office, or a guesthouse. Challenge yourself to plan it with thoughtful storage solutions and ways to easily transition from day to night or from business hours to after-hours: a bench seat can double as storage, a loft space accommodates sleeping, and a table or desk can transform into a bar or countertop. When designing or commissioning built-ins, be conscious of your height in relation to the piece's intended function: Make it custom for you and the way you live, rather than just going off of standardized measurements.

Mason's Los Feliz clients initially wanted to remodel their garage, an original carriage house painted baby blue with white trim. Instead, Mason suggested simply painting it one color—Turkish Coffee by Valspar (the same shade we used on the exterior of our Topanga house)—transforming it into a sort of object.

CHAPTER SIX

NESTING

For a long time, we dreamed of a handmade dining room table: a table consisting of an organically complex and elegant rectangular slab of walnut specially sourced for the project from Evan, our wood broker, with custom-designed curved brass legs.

Stylistically, our current dining table is a world away from that table: It is a modern white powder-coated steel piece from Blu Dot with a triangular base. It's a table we initially brought down from San Francisco out of necessity when we first moved in: Serena—four months pregnant at the time—was working on her largest commission to date, a ten-foot-long mural for San Francisco restaurant Tartine Manufactory, and we needed a place to spread out.

The table transformed the dining room into her art studio and, when cleared, became the place for us to gather and break bread as our house took shape around us. In a sense, this table is holding the space for the fantasy version we cannot currently afford.

Even so, we've fallen a little bit in love with this placeholder: its clean lines, its sturdiness, its utility—the way it blends seamlessly with its surroundings and is both modular and easy to clean. It functions in a way that supports Serena's art practice, and so, for however long it takes for us to get her a dedicated studio, this is our table.

Our house is a multifunctional space at all times. When you're making decisions, be sure to choose things that aren't too precious to be used. Our Ramsey Conder light, for example, sometimes doubles as a laundry drying rack.

It's important to remember that the nesting process is an organic, imperfect, and ever-evolving one. There is no single right way to approach it, but for us, the most effective jumping-off point is determining the space's dominant piece.

In all likelihood, this piece is the thing that occupies the most real estate in the room, and it's also the thing that's emblematic of the room's purpose—the dining room's dining table, the living room's sofa, the bedroom's bed.

With this starting point in place, you can nail down the pieces that will orbit around it, considering your must-haves and assigning each to a location (be it the family heirloom armoire, the bookshelves or desk, the coffee table or lounge chair).

In the case of our dining room, we could not move forward in the space, or with our lives, really, without finding something that addressed our needs. Holding out for "the one" would have been a counterproductive pursuit. And yet, it's worth doing the research and knowing what that "one" thing is, both so that you have a vision for your ultimate goal, and so that you can make a conscious decision as to the piece you eventually decide to pursue in place of your "reach piece," and why.

We knew we wanted a long, rectangular table to shape the room, something maneuverable and not too bulky, so as not to interrupt the sight lines, in a versatile neutral color and a hard-wearing material too. These are qualities that any table we put here will possess, offering us the versatility to grow and change, without rendering the entire room in disarray.

Serena's studio with art-supply storage is on the porch, safely out of Wild's reach.
Everything has a place, thanks to a custom wooden shelf by Danny Montoya.

A pitcher by Robert Blue. Opposite: Ceramics for days in General Store Venice

A WORD ABOUT FOCAL POINTS

We make a distinction between a room's orientation and its focal point: As we mentioned earlier, when possible we like to orient a room toward the window, encouraging people in the space to direct their attention that way by positioning furniture so that it faces the outside.

A focal point—the place your eye travels to first in a space and wants to linger on—can translate to different objects, depending on your position in a space. We try to make it so that whatever direction you turn in a room, you're met with a compelling focal point, whether it happens to be the windows, a wall hanging, the fireplace, or something else entirely.

In a perfect world, the focal point should be one of your favorite things in the space—the thing that is a reflection of you and holds personal meaning. Your room's focal point and its dominant piece aren't necessarily one and the same, though they can be.

Our Paul McCobb–style midcentury bookshelf and Dieter Rams turntable are nice to look at, sure, but the real focal point is the view behind them.

Your focal point is sometimes elusive, revealing itself to you only once the rest of the room has been placed (as with our Heather Levine wall hanging, which is installed above our sofa and was quite literally the finishing touch). It can also be a strategic addition, as in our kitchen's floating shelves, which were painstakingly envisioned and showcase a lifetime of collected treasures alongside beautiful, useful items.

If you are wedded to a specific focal point from the get-go—say, it's the only thing you know for absolutely sure that you want to include in a space when you begin to conceptualize or redesign a room—you can of course approach the layout from this standpoint, select the dominant piece next, in conversation with it, and so on from there.

The takeaway? You need someplace to start—an anchor—to prevent you from creating a puzzle whose pieces don't fit.

From top: At Mason's midcentury residential project in Topanga, the kitchen makes the most of the ultimate dishwashing vista. When telephone lines get in the way of your view, as is the case in our Irving Street apartment, orient toward beauty inside, like this Heather Levine wall hanging.

"Our Thonet rocking chair was one of those things I'd wanted for a long time, but I was waiting for the moment when it would have a place in my life—it's harder to justify a rocking chair purchase when you're younger—and then it did. I can't remember if I was pregnant at the time, or just hoping to be, but we went to the Santa Monica Airport Antique and Collectible Market and found it there." —SMM

A fireplace makes for not only a natural focal point but also an opportunity to create vignettes on its mantel. In our Great Highway apartment in San Francisco, a painting by Michelle Blade shares space with a J. B. Blunk cup, a wooden hand, and other odds and ends.

TAKING STOCK

By the time most people reach an age where they are thinking about decorating a room, they will have accumulated a collection of things. As we've already mentioned, reenvisioning a room does not mean getting rid of everything you own, but rather reassessing, recategorizing, and editing your belongings—eliminating anything that no longer serves you, and gradually replacing the pieces that are no longer compatible with your lifestyle, your surroundings, or your aesthetic.

Ridding yourself of superfluous things will allow a clear picture of the "holes"—places where you want to add or replace items—and also make it easier to rearrange your space to uncover an ideal layout (a lesson Mason learned at a young age from his mom, who would change up the positioning of the furniture while he was at school, so that he came home to find an entirely new, yet familiar, environment).

Mason made the desk in our Great Highway apartment ten years ago from unfinished plywood. We always like the effect of mixing modern and vintage, so we paired it with a Cherner chair.

FINDING THE THINGS

You have to know what you're looking for. Because it is our passion and livelihood, we have spent countless hours educating ourselves on the repertoires of Paul McCobb, Donald Judd, Charles and Ray Eames, Nanna Ditzel, Jean Prouvé, Greta Grossman, Florence Knoll, and many others. Pinterest boards, shelter magazines, and coffee-table books may help you become attuned to the things that appeal. And the online marketplace 1stdibs is a great place to delve deeper into design masters, the history of craftsmanship, and ways to identify authentic pieces, as is eBay.

It's also important to think about scale—regardless of a piece's allure, if it's too large for the room for which it's intended, it will dwarf the space, thwarting the overall effect. If it's too small, it can result in the space feeling lonely or uninviting.

For us, finding furniture typically starts at the flea markets and our favorite thrift stores. If those don't yield results, we move on to online classifieds. Wherever possible, we try to buy used or vintage before buying new: For us, it is the ultimate form of recycling, ensuring that our home is filled with history and that, because of our choice, there will be one less thing that ends up in a landfill. It doesn't hurt that we also happen to love the look of something well-worn, with visible patina.

If your search doesn't lead you to the right piece, and you don't have the time or desire to continue down this path, consider taking a leap of faith and sitting down with a craftsperson to try to make the piece in an affordable way that suits your budget. When we do buy new, it's important to us to feel confident that the piece is well made and will last.

Serena recently came across this dresser at a flea market; it called to her with its brass feet, circular handles, and half-circle pulls. It's also not in perfect condition, which in Serena's book is a plus.

A Word About Flea Markets

You can't go to a flea market with the sole goal of finding one specific thing. Instead, you need to keep a mental watch list of your dream pieces and your budget for each of these things handy, so that when you do encounter one of them, you will recognize it, know its worth, and be ready. (On the subject of price, when the seller gives you a number, if it falls within your mental range, it's worth attempting to talk the seller down a bit. However, if the opening figure is five times what you want to spend, be prepared to walk away.)

Becoming a regular also pays off: You increase your chances of finding what you're looking for, expand your understanding of available inventory, and often become friendly with vendors who can keep an eye out for you.

Finally, when you do find something that fits what you are looking for, be sure to assess its integrity by trying it out: If it's a desk, open the drawers and shake them around; if it's a chair, sit in it; if it's a table and has folding sides, fold them—you get the idea. Look at it from all angles for evidence of breaks and repairs, and look underneath for signatures and dates that back up what it purports to be. You want to feel and look at every bit of it and know what you're getting. That said, don't be hung up on finding something that's "a name"—it doesn't have to be an Eames chair to be a treasure.

THE MIX

The things that populate our Topanga home and our flat in San Francisco represent a sort of map of our lives and our tastes, hailing from all over the world and spanning the new, used, and vintage—from the aforementioned industrial Blu Dot Strut studio table and our Modernica Case Study Daybed, to our Paul McCobb spindle-back chairs and Saarinen tulip table.

There is no single formula to ensure cohesion, but for us, maintaining a palette of neutrals and consistent wood tones results in a scheme in which things "play" well together. There is a common thread. That same theory can be extrapolated to include your particular chosen themes and motifs; whether it's florals or modern Zen, blending is successful so long as you have recurring, consistent elements. In other words, balance difference with sameness.

In the breakfast nook of our Great Highway apartment, an Alvar Aalto table is set with a Paul McCobb chair, but also a rattan stool from the flea market—to maintain the mix and keep things from being exclusively midcentury.

The living room of our Great Highway apartment, where a Modernica couch pairs nicely with a chunk of wood that serves as our coffee table.

CRAFTS DESIGN

CRAFTING A MODERN WORLD

CHAPTER SEVEN

ADORNMENT

Nearly all of the handcrafted goods you'll find in our house are made by people with whom we have personal relationships: the mugs that we drink our coffee out of (created by makers including Kat & Roger and Humble Ceramics), the Victoria Morris lamps in our bedroom, and the Ramsey Conder toilet scrubber holder in our bathroom.

Yes, we do have a hand-forged brass vessel to hold our (wood) toilet scrubber. It's high on the list of best household purchases we've ever made. And we realize that people who are skeptical of our lifestyle may find this ridiculous. But think about it: Is there anything better to spend your disposable income on than an everyday object you will use forever that elevates one of life's more unsavory tasks to something beautiful and replaces the need for something plastic and disposable that will inevitably end up in a landfill?

A Paul McCobb desk paired with a midcentury stool makes for a quiet vignette in the corner of our Topanga living room. A painting by Jessica Niello-White hangs below a hawk feather Mason stuck in a knothole in the wood. (The hawk is Mason's spirit animal.)

These are the kinds of finishing touches that set your home apart from others. There's ample opportunity for function and beauty to overlap, from area rugs to doorknobs. But there's also room for beauty for beauty's sake—objects that are a pleasure to behold, and plants whose very presence bolsters your mood.

This is the reason we don't have a sales-forward approach in our stores. We always tell our employees that it's most important to us that people have a good experience, and that they really understand what it is that they're looking at—who made it, and how. Ultimately, we want people to walk out the door saying, "I bought this thing because I love it and I love the story behind it."

The key is to edit thoughtfully: find the things you not only like, but also want to spend every day with—things that enhance your surroundings rather than compete for attention with them.

Adornment in action: from the telephone nook in our Great Highway apartment—populated with a vintage painting, a crystal from Serena's mom, and a glass vase from Japan—to our ever-expanding collection of mugs

"I buy tons of kitchen stuff that is beautiful but not necessary. I have a brass container that holds tea and coffee— my coffee is fine in its coffee bag, but I don't like to look at the coffee bag. I also asked our friend Mike Beavers to make me a wooden box to hold my Chemex filters. I find it so satisfying to look at this simple, beautiful box every day. And I wouldn't get that satisfaction from looking at the cardboard box that the filters come in." –SMM

A Mount Washington vase, Heather Levine wall hanging, vintage candleholder, and light switch cover from Mexico turn an empty corner into a one-of-a-kind vignette. Opposite: Serena collects hats to display as a decorative element as well as to wear.

A wood wall hanging by Katie Gong pulls focus in the kitchen of Mason's Noe Valley project. A sculptural piece of art from the homeowner's private collection hangs above the dining table, set with Alvar Aalto chairs.

LIGHTING

Think of lamps, chandeliers, pendants, and sconces as functional sculpture: They should be beautiful, and the light has to work well in its intended space. (A single-bulb fixture over your dining room table may be elegant, but if you can't see your food by its glow, it's useless.)

Choosing the right bulb is another crucial consideration: LED bulbs are most energy-efficient, and they've evolved to the point that some produce a similar light to that of an incandescent bulb (our guilty favorite), if not identical. Manufacturers use all sorts of language to describe a bulb's effect—soft, warm, etcetera—but the bottom line is that you're best off choosing a bulb whose glow is as close to natural light as possible. To take out the guesswork, you can visit a lighting showroom where you can see your options in use and avoid the expensive trial and error of buying lightbulbs that you might never return.

We chose this simple marble and brass lamp for our bedside not only because of its use of material but also for its distinct shape. Its low profile leaves just enough room for a glass of water.

We found a Kurt Versen standing lamp that we both loved, so we decided to skip the nightstands in the bedroom of our Great Highway apartment and make the most of the low bed height. A piece by Robin Bright points the way to sleep.

Table Lamps

We're drawn to table lamps with ceramic and wood bases, in line with the materials we use throughout our home. For the bedside, we tend to look for smaller lamps so as not to overwhelm the space and to leave room for books, water carafes, or other items that need to be within arm's reach.

When choosing a shade, keep in mind that it should completely cover the lamp's hardware and socket, leaving the neck visible—it's preferable aesthetically, and also helps to ensure the shade will properly distribute the light. Keep in mind too that a lighter shade will distribute the light more evenly.

Floor Lamps

A floor lamp tends to work best in a spacious room in which it serves as the focal point—it requires a substantial base to be structurally sound and, given its size, often functions as a piece of furniture in its own right. Be sure to consider the height of the floor lamp's light—when sitting on a sofa, for example, you don't want to be at eye level with the bulb.

Pendants and Chandeliers

A suspended light makes for a dramatic statement over a dining or worktable, in a hallway or entryway, in a den, or over a bed in a bedroom if you have high ceilings. Before buying or installing, be sure to determine the optimum height in the space you have in mind for your fixture to confirm that its dimensions are compatible ahead of time—too low and you risk hitting your head, too high and the light may not illuminate the space evenly.

Ceiling Mounts

If you have low ceilings, you're better off skipping the pendant or chandelier option and doing a ceiling mount, which will ensure that your light is distributed evenly (and that the fixture itself doesn't get in your way). In this scenario we like a more traditional surface mount in the form of a glass sphere, a flat glass cylinder, or a flush-mount drum.

First row, from left: Noguchi Akari pendant light, Ramsey Conder custom brass chandelier, Heather Levine ceramic pendants. Second row: Victoria Morris XL White Thimble lamp, vintage floor lamps, Ramsey Conder three-arm articulating lamp. Third row: midcentury glass globe pendant, Victoria Morris Carved Arch Thimble lamp, Ramsey Conder surface-mount ceiling lamp

"I am drawn to very simple, functional lighting that incorporates elements of shapes, whether it's a table lamp with decorative triangular cutouts or sconces with perfectly circular switch knobs." —SMM

Sconces

When surface, floor, and ceiling space is limited, sconces are ideal. Their placement is important—if they are installed as a pair over bedside tables, in a bathroom, or outside on either side of your door, take care to be sure they are even. You also don't want to put them in an area where they will get in your way, so pick a place that's out of foot traffic and/or high enough that you won't bump into them.

Our favorites: porcelain sockets fitted with bare or brass-dipped bulbs, Ramsey Conder flat brass round plates that mount directly to the wall, and, space permitting, the Prouvé Potence lamp.

LAYERING

We were both raised with an appreciation for textiles. In high school in Hawaii, Serena hunted with her mom for bold, colorful sixties and seventies–era fabrics from which to make tote bags; Mason grew up with a natural familiarity with Navajo blankets, thanks to his family's Native American ancestry.

It was also a common denominator early in our relationship, when, on a trip to New York, we got to know each other better while searching for fabric in Harlem. It's become a tradition for us when visiting new places to check out the fabric stores and markets there—textiles represent a connection to cultural exploration, warmth, and home.

This is not what we mean by layering, but it is real.

Pillows and Blankets

Our home is a haven for pillows. At most recent count, there are four throw pillows (ranging from linen to vintage to hand-embroidered from Mexico) on our sofa, five linen floor pillows on the floor (each durable and washable, used both for lounging and for our dog, Macie, and our cat, Nemo), and seven on the bed—all used for sleeping—including a body pillow that was introduced while Serena was pregnant and hasn't left since.

What's with all the pillows? There's something about their abundance that infuses a bit of luxury and indulgence into your daily existence. They warm up the space with their soft tactility and, given the shades-of-white palette our personal collection adheres to, create a peaceful, textured landscape that blends seamlessly and offers organic opportunities for repose.

We only introduce pillows that we actually use—no need for stiff, decorative bolsters on the bed that need to be stored elsewhere while you sleep, or overly ornate accents on the sofa that infringe on guests' comfort rather than increasing it.

Open our linen closet and you'll find a collection of family quilts and heirloom blankets, an assortment of homespun one-offs picked up at flea markets, a century-old indigo blanket Serena discovered at the Brimfield Antique Flea Market in Massachusetts, and a wool khadi throw from Indian textile source Auntie Oti, to name but a few.

Some of these things have been with us our whole lives, and we are constantly adding to the collection. We love the thrill of hunting and collecting, and throws and blankets are easily stored, handy to swap in and out when temperatures change or something gets dirty, and a necessity when we have houseguests. Having a bounty is never a bad thing.

When blending patterns and styles, a good rule of thumb is to keep some element of uniformity: This mix of early American homespun textiles, General Store linen pillows, and a khadi pillow and a Hawaiian quilted pillow plays well together thanks to a monochromatic palette.

Rugs

The bohemian look of rugs overlapping on rugs overlapping on rugs for a maximalist wow statement continues to be popular, yet we tend to use floor coverings sparingly and strategically: to warm up a space, cut down on noise, or fill the need for a soft spot for gathering.

A handwoven, faded Moroccan throw rug lies at the base of our bed, cushioning the floor for our dog, Macie, as she jumps on and off throughout the night; a vintage Berber-style Moroccan rug in Wild's room encompasses his play area; and a woven Turkish hemp kilim ties together the living room.

When buying rugs, we tend to look for those that balance intricate pattern with a calming muted palette or display a rare color or pattern combination: Persian and Navajo rugs with blue and brown tones, vintage Moroccan rugs spanning Berber to Beni Ourain and beyond, and Central and South American rugs with a monochromatic palette are always on our radar. Rugs that are more than a hundred years old tend to be more interesting, utilizing natural dyes and wool and cotton as opposed to synthetic colors and polyester blends.

This vintage Moroccan hand-woven Berber Azilal rug is evidence we can embrace bold colors.

BUYING A RUG

Measure your space ahead of time. Putting down blue tape that matches the rug dimensions you're considering will help you to fully understand how much of an area you want to cover and make decisions about whether you want your furniture to live on top of the rug or outside of it (better to choose one or the other than to fall into a halfway on-and-off setup).

When shopping online for rugs, request additional photos of the piece in indoor and outdoor lighting to get the best possible understanding of the rug's true colors. Check the return policy too, as a rug will always look different in person.

Make sure you are buying something that you're actually going to use: If a rug is so precious and expensive that you don't feel comfortable walking on it, then there's not much point in making the investment (unless you plan to hang it on the wall).

Finally, buy something that feels good. We love the look of natural fibers like hemp and jute, but it's important to make sure that they're not so tough on your skin that you have an aversion to living with them.

FIXTURES

We adhere to a palette of mostly natural untreated brass for our fixtures; it connotes a time-tested sturdiness—like they've been there forever, and are still a pleasure to use. Keeping the material uniform, from drawer pulls to faucets to doorknobs, hooks, and hinges, acts as a unifying thread in your design scheme. When buying fixtures en masse, it's best to start with the things that are the hardest to find—often the kitchen or shower faucets—and then try to loosely match your other fixtures to them.

We looked everywhere for the perfect faucet for the kitchen and finally ended up importing a deVOL aged brass tap by Perrin and Rowe from England. When you're choosing something as hardworking as this, make sure to take into account its functionality: This faucet looks good, but also swivels, sits up high, and is a pleasure to use.

ON THE WALLS

Let's start with wall hangings, which are a must for us. The category has become increasingly trendy—from macramé to dip-dyed weavings—but we favor tactile, modern, sculptural pieces composed of sturdy, lasting materials.

The work of Heather Levine is a case in point, recurring throughout our homes and projects; her geometric sandstone and branch creations integrate seamlessly and work as focal points. We also love Mt. Washington Pottery ceramic bells, hand-carved by founder Beth Katz—which are installed in our fireplace and look fantastic hanging in nooks or on a porch. And stained-glass wall hangings like those made by David Scheid double as art and light catchers when hung in or next to a window.

The walls in our homes in San Francisco and Topanga feature pieces spanning from vintage seascapes to oil paintings to photographs by artist friends and family (Andrew Paynter, Daren Wilson, Paul Wackers, Thomas Campbell, Hilary Pecis, Kyle Field, Michelle Blade, Clare Rojas, Chris Gentile, Orion Shepherd, and Serena's mom, Susan Mitnik, among them). They all resonate on a deeper personal level, which ensures that we never tire of looking at them.

Each piece is framed in natural wood with as minimal a profile as possible and without formal mat treatments. For larger pieces we prefer ample wall space in order to let them breathe, rather than overcrowding with other works. For the smaller ones, we cluster them together for a larger impact, creating the effect that they comprise one large piece.

Our friend Paul Wackers traded one of his pieces (painted on a wood panel so it didn't need a frame) for one of Serena's. We mounted it across from a window in our Great Highway apartment, and since it's one of our larger paintings, it fits the space well on its own.

A David Wilson drawing hangs over the bed in Bay Abode, our new San Francisco rental property. We bought the piece at a show at Mollusk years ago, and it's extra meaningful because it depicts the dunes in front of our Great Highway apartment. A pair of vintage alabaster lamps serves as reading lights.

OBJECTS

Try as we might to keep clutter at bay, we have a habit of amassing things whose sole use is to provide enjoyment: Heidi Anderson totems, Ido Yoshimoto wood objects, Rebekah Miles miniature vases, and Daren Wilson pinch pots among them. We install these keepsakes in places where they can provide delight without infringing on useful space: positioning items on the tip-top of a bookshelf or the very corner of a countertop, or grouping objects in a vintage basket underneath the coffee table.

When we look at, talk about, or touch these objects, it makes us think about the people behind them—many of them friends who are important in our lives, and some whom we don't get to see all that often. Besides their beauty, these objects also keep us connected to their makers, which is more fulfilling than just having things for the sake of it.

In our Irving Street location of General Store, a circular shelving unit in the wall is an object to behold in its own right. Collecting all of your objects in one area makes for a powerful display, as opposed to scattering them all over the place, which can end up reading as cluttered.

A few of our favorite things, including a Mt. Washington
ceramic, a piece by Serena, a lifeguard stand model by
Chris Gentile, and a vase by Victoria Morris

Modern Originals   AT HOME WITH MIDCENTURY
                    EUROPEAN DESIGNERS

The Plant magazine   The appearance will become the reality   12

Georgia O'Keeffe   Art and Letters

PLANT LIFE

Our not-at-all-scientific approach to decorating with plants is this: Add a plant anywhere that looks lonely. Beyond that stipulation, we like to group plants in areas that aren't being otherwise utilized (say, the hearth of a nonfunctional fireplace), in the corners of the room (a great spot for larger plants), and anywhere you would otherwise put an object (a side table, next to the sink, on a nightstand, a windowsill, or a shelf), plus less expected places like the top of the fridge.

   As with outdoor landscaping, it's important to know your abilities and lighting limitations when it comes to nurturing living things inside. We often default to more foolproof plants like succulents, housed in simplistic ceramic or concrete planters—including midcentury classics from Architectural Pottery, Bauer, and Gainey.

Serena collects vintage ceramics in varying sizes, shapes, and shades of white and plants each with a different type of plant to keep it visually interesting.

Art in the form of planters, from left: vintage, Mount Washington,
Heidi Anderson, vintage, Question of Eagles, Julie Cloutier

CHAPTER EIGHT

LIVING

The very first gathering we ever had at our Topanga home took place right after we had finished whitewashing the floors and painting the walls. The bathroom still wasn't done, there was no kitchen, and there was no furniture, save for a couple of thrift store chairs. There wasn't even a driveway. And to complicate matters, it was raining (in Southern California!).

At the time, we were also living in separate cities—Serena was based mostly full-time in Topanga, while Mason was back and forth between San Francisco and L.A. on a weekly basis, working in Sausalito for architect Phil Rossington.

Everything was in progress. But we were both like: We bought a house! Let's have some people over.

We dragged our camper mattress from the bedroom to the living room—which was easy since we didn't have a wall between the two rooms—so that people would have somewhere to sit. Mason made a nineties indie rock playlist and everyone brought food, wine, and beer for a potluck. Some people knew each other and some people didn't: Friendships were struck (through mutual creative appreciation, and more niche topics, like sprinter vans) as the kids ran laps in the empty house.

For a couple of hours the downpour turned torrential—with all of the windows open and the muggy air wafting through the house, it added a tangible thrill to the proceedings.

Even with the house in disarray, and even with some cars getting seriously stuck in the mud, the party was a huge success. Who needed furniture with friends like these? For us, it underlined what we love about the process of building out and designing a space: Things are never perfect, things are never done, and the evidence of life is an integral part of a home's story and its innate beauty.

Nearly two years later, we celebrated Wild's first birthday here, with many of the same faces and some new. We had come a long way since then—we had a door on the bathroom, for starters, a driveway, a finished deck, and a kitchen, and all of the rooms were, from the looks of things, complete.

But there was still a full to-do list: Our much-anticipated freestanding and self-supporting shelf for the dining area hadn't yet been designed, we didn't yet have A/C or heating, and there was a ton of landscaping still to be done, including planting our fruit tree orchard.

A casual end-of-summer gathering with the friends we call family: Jess Bianchi-Mau, Malia Bianchi-Mau, and their son Okana, John Moore, Hannah Henderson with their son Costa, Mike and Charlotte Beavers, and Brian Dow. The occasion? To break in our new outdoor table by Mike Beavers with a feast of summer rolls, gluten-free pistachio rose tarts, crudités, and more by the talented Lori Stern.

Because, this time, it was a sunny day, we set out pillows and rugs on the deck, so people could gather there while the kids played in the yard. Inside, our faithful Strut table held a Mediterranean buffet full of mezze delicacies as friends reconnected and sat with filled plates on the sofa and the floor.

The house had officially gone from being our nest to being Wild's home, as evidenced by a scattering of wood toys, the absence of low-lying breakables, and the toucan and rainbow piñatas strung up outside for the occasion. (Never mind that we didn't own a baseball bat and had to borrow one from a neighbor.)

Hours later, after everyone had left, the floors were filthy, piñata debris and rogue pieces of candy were scattered outside, and the vintage caning on our Thonet rocking chair, which, fittingly, was the first piece of furniture we bought after finding out Serena was pregnant with Wild, had finally given way. All of it, Thonet chair included, is the price you pay for having fun and living—the reason you have a space that's yours in the first place—and it's more than okay with us.

We know it doesn't look this way on Instagram, but even before Wild came along, and especially since then, our house is a mess—a beautiful mess—pretty much all of the time. After three years living in our beautiful mess, we have a new store in San Francisco and a new rental property, we've expanded our store in Venice, and Serena is pregnant again, this time with a girl.

Which means it's time for a new project: dreaming up plans for an additional bedroom and a studio for our expanding family.

We are always looking forward. But the thing that keeps us inspired is the process of getting there—we have an intuitive desire to do what we do. And while this may not be the case for you, if there's one thing we hope this book will leave you with, it's this: Whenever possible, don't be discouraged to dream. Think about your space and how you can make it better: Don't let fear of failing stop you from installing a shelf or ripping up a carpet. Try not to take it too seriously—try to be light about it. Because if it means that it will make your life better and more beautiful while you're living in the space you occupy, there is no downside.

This is what it's all about: making a space that is warm and inviting and comfortable and sharing it with your family and friends. It's all we could ever hope for.

Acknowledgments:

We would like to thank our parents, family, and friends for always being there for us with love and support no matter the circumstance.

Thank you to all at Abrams, including Holly Dolce, Sarah Massey, and the rest of the team. This book could not have been possible without Katherine "Kitty" Cowles, whose idea it was for us to make a book. And, most important, our team: writer Melissa Goldstein, photographer Mariko Reed, and designer Jeff Canham; without these talents there would be no book.

Thank you to the General Store family in San Francisco and Venice, especially our partners in Venice, Hannah Henderson and John Moore, for believing in and supporting us since the beginning.

Thank you to Lori Stern for cooking the delicious and nourishing food captured in the "Living" chapter. Extra-special thanks to Rachel Barrett, Josh Kessler, Beatrice Faverjon, Andrea Shapiro, Naya Peterson, Oliver Fross, Birgit Sfat, Raul Sfat, Jess Bianchi-Mau, and Malia Bianchi-Mau, who let us photograph their homes, designed by Mason.

Last but not least, to our children; you are everything to us and the sole purpose for creating our Abode.

Editors: Holly Dolce and Sarah Massey
Photographer: Mariko Reed
Designer: Jeff Canham
Production Manager: Denise LaCongo
Illustrations: Mason St. Peter
Watercolor paintings: Serena Mitnik-Miller
Photographs of watercolors: JW White / Phocasso
Photographs on pages 10, 15, 22, 28: SMM and MSP

MSP Design Inc. projects:
Berkeley: pages 80–81
Great Highway: pages 58–59, 119, 130
Los Feliz: pages 57, 72–73, 103, 137–139, 164–165
Mar Vista 1: pages 144–145
Mar Vista 2: page 28 (lower left)
Noe Valley: pages 83, 154–155, 210–211
Topanga Mid-Century project: page 181 (top photo)

Landscape design by Eric Brandon Gomez: pages 144–145
Fence built and additional design by Tim Wolff and Raul Sfat: pages 154–155

Library of Congress Control Number: 2018936260

ISBN: 978-1-4197-3454-0
eISBN: 978-1-68335-511-3

Text copyright © 2019 Serena Mitnik-Miller and Mason St. Peter
Photographs copyright © 2019 Mariko Reed

Jacket © 2019 Abrams

Printed and bound in China
10 9 8 7 6 5 4 3 2 1

Abrams books are available at special discounts when purchased in quantity for premiums and promotions as well as fundraising or educational use. Special editions can also be created to specification. For details, contact specialsales@abramsbooks.com or the address below.

Abrams® is a registered trademark of Harry N. Abrams, Inc.

ABRAMS
The Art of Books

195 Broadway
New York, NY 10007
abramsbooks.com